Truly's Special Birthday

Halley Tells Her Story

Farm Photo Book #2

By

Donna Lindahl - St. Dennis

ISBN-13: 978-1535169288
ISBN-10: 1535169281

Copyright © 2016 by Donna Lindahl – St. Dennis. No part of this book may be reproduced in any form or format without written permission from the author.

April 17

is Truly's Birthday.

In this Farm Photo Book

Halley tells the story about

her Mama Truly's

special birthday present.

Hi!

My name is Halley.

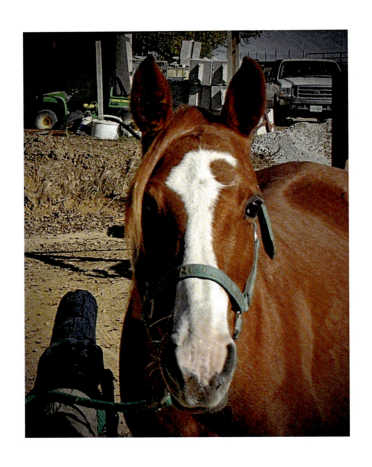

This is my mama.

Her name is Truly.

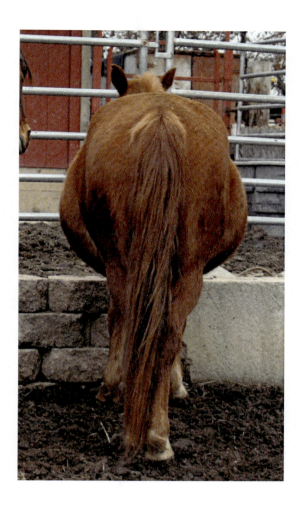

When my Mama Truly

was pregnant with me,

her tummy was big!

Mama Truly knew

that her birthday

would be special.

She had a surprise.

It would be my birthday too!

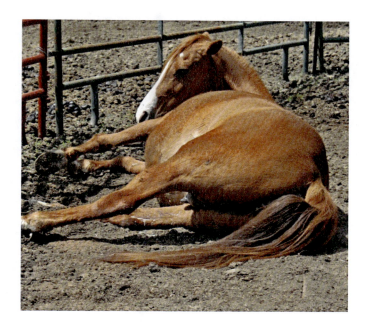

Mama Truly got ready.

After I was born,

Mama Truly reached around

and gave me a nose kiss.

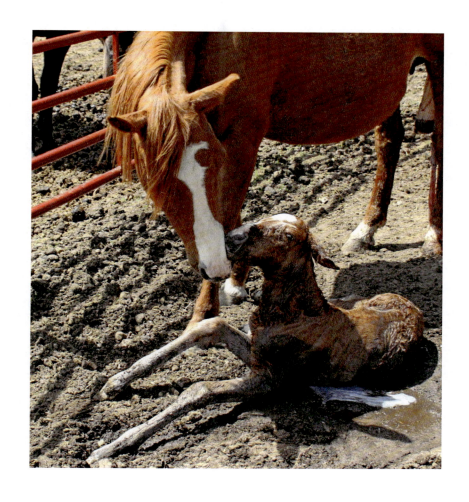

My ears were floppy and I couldn't see.

Mama Truly made me feel safe.

She let me smell her face.

Then she raised her head

and made a happy whinny.

My big brother, Charm, watched

from outside the fence.

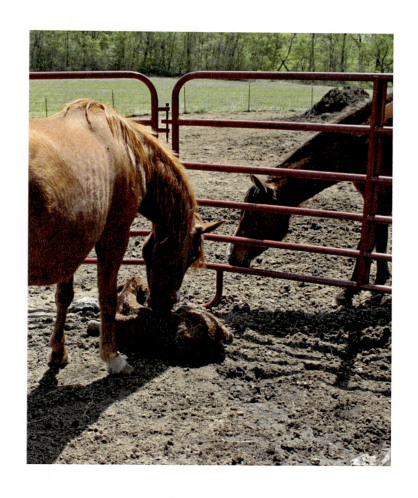

Mama Truly licked me

to dry my hair and give me energy.

It was time for me to stand up.

Mama Truly put her nose under my chin and pushed me gently.

Yeah!

I got my feet under me.

I stood up

all by my self!

But when I tried to walk

my feet got mixed up.

I fell over.

I fell too close to the fence.

Big brother Charm couldn't help me.

Mama Truly couldn't help me.

I was stuck!

I needed help

from a friend.

Friend, Gary, carefully helped me stand up again.

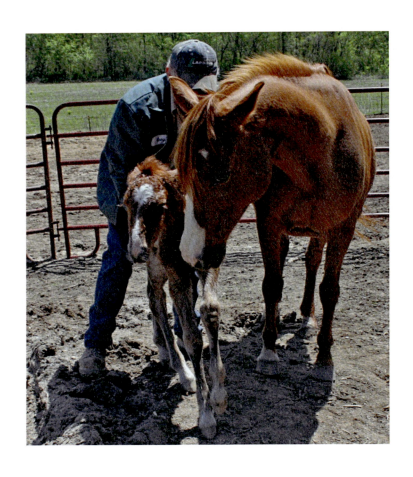

Gary helped me walk.

Mama Truly stayed

close beside me.

Finally I was in a safe place

far away from the fence.

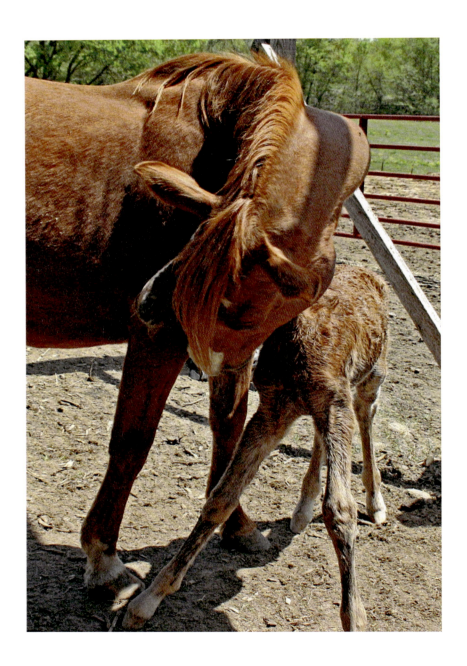

Mama Truly gave me a big hug.

Then she licked me

and rubbed me all over

with her nose.

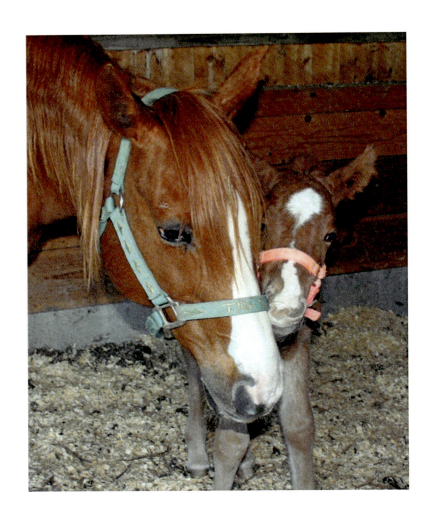

Gary put a tiny pink halter

on my head.

He said it was Mama Truly's

very own baby halter!

I thanked Gary

for helping me walk.

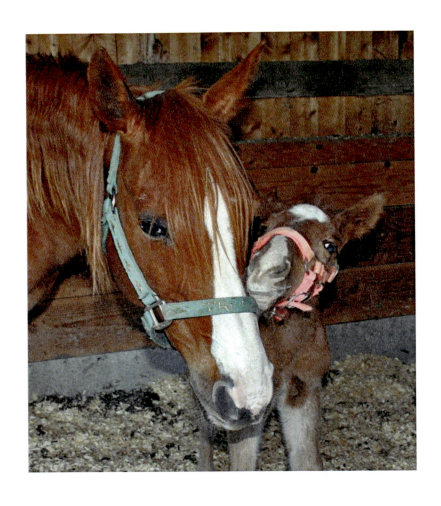

And I thanked

Mama Truly for being my

very special birthday mama!

Made in the USA
San Bernardino, CA
11 July 2016